Live
Poets
Society

Ndidi,

Enjoy the book

Thx 4 supporting

God Bless

Cocktails

Author & Editor: E. Christopher Cornell
Layout & Design: Erica M. Corbett, Mad Cartoonist, Inc.

Manufactured in the United States of America

ISBN 0-615-13061-5

For more information:

E. Christopher Cornell
Live Poets Society, L.L.C.
3354 Springside Ridge
Decatur, GA 30034
elluin@bellsouth.net

Log on to receive the weekly commentaries
www.livepoets.net

Cocktails Commentary:

Volume I

by
E. Christopher Cornell
a.k.a.
Cocktails

CONTENTS

Foreword

Fear. Uncertainty. Procrastination. Confidence. Arrogance. I can write better than them. Wow, they are really good. Long Time Coming. It's About Time. What are you waiting for? Me an author? I'm a writer, have been writing all my life. I've been writing these commentaries for five solid years, two to three times a week. Why now? Why not?

These are the thoughts that run through my head on a daily basis. I thank God for my gift. It is His way of maintaining my sanity. True, I think I'm WAY MORE stable than a lot of artists that I meet. Not a knock on authors and artists, but I really don't consider myself eclectic. I am a conservative liberal. I hate boundaries, but draw them for myself. This compilation of commentaries is the first of hopefully many volumes. As long as you read them, I will keep cranking them out.

This is not your traditional poetry book. Sentence structure wise, format, grammar, and timelines have been blurred. I write like I talk, so hopefully if you have heard my voice, picture it in your head. If you've never heard me speak before, read it in your voice. The important thing is this body of work is OUR voice. The reason that I was encouraged to keep writing these commentaries is because people would email me back, and express gratitude for helping them make it through the day. That blew me away. Just my thoughts, or so I thought. What I was thinking at the time tran-scended paper and email and touched hearts and souls. Once God reveals something, you can't act like it's not there. A lot of people think that this book should have been finished sooner. But the spirit on me is telling me it's right on time.

Me being Cocktails, I had to add my own twist. So before each chapter I have provided a drink recipe for your experimentation and party pleasure. If you are a youth reading this (18 and younger), my disclaimer is that drugs and alcohol are bad. There is a time and a place for everything, and it's called college. Just jokes...maybe. Please open your hearts, minds, and souls while you peruse these pages. For you are about to jump in my ear and crawl through my mind. Thanks for your support and purchase. Holla at ya boy!

E. Christopher "Cocktails" Cornell
Co-Founder
Live Poets Society, L.L.C.
www.livepoets.net

7

Chapter 1
Drink 1

The Dating Game

Foreplay on Neutral Ground

Ingredients

8 oz Absolut Vodka, 4 oz Midori Melon Liqueur, 12 oz Pineapple Juice, 12 oz Cranberry Juice and Ice

Mixing Instructions

Fill glasses with ice. Mix Absolut, Midori, Pineapple juice and Cranberry juice in a decanter. Pour over ice and serve. Makes several servings.

HELLO

Hello.

I'm sorry to disturb you so late, but this couldn't wait. I haven't stopped thinking about you since our last date. Compared to your other suitors, I was trying to figure out how I rate. I'm calm under pressure, while these others guys get so irate. Do you believe in fate? What do you look for when you choose your mate? Make no mistake. I would hate to be a burden on your future plans. Do you believe in love at first sight, or do I have to walk by again? We could walk by land, swinging arms, hand in hand. I'm trying to formulate the words to make you understand. You are the stitching in my fabric of a man. If no one else can do it, trust me I can. Because I truly am missing you. I can't stop thinking about kissing you. And I am hoping and wishing you feel the same. When I left your doorstep, I haven't felt the same. I'm tired of playing this game. I'm looking for stability, In His Name. We have nothing to lose and everything to gain. So I will make this simple and plain. When can I see you again. This is Cocktails coming from my passion and poetry home cubicle. Be honest in relationships.

TEMPTATION

Dear God,

I've been having an inner struggle. In my last attempt to snuggle, our lustful tussle found myself in her inner muscle. I was the cock in her hen house and my feathers began to rustle. When we finished the room looked like there had been a scuffle. I'm a repeat offender with this inner trouble. I know that my jagged edges are but one piece of the puzzle, so I hope my prayer doesn't get lost in the hustle and bustle. And by the way, I think my hustle is busted, because my thinking wheel is rusted. My new concepts seem old, and I'm becoming disgusted. Which scares me because my opinion is trusted, and what I'm thinking will have someone's life adjusted. I hope that this spiritual archaeological dig won't find my sarcophagus dusted. Because that means someone raided my tomb, and my thoughts of raiding wombs are seeds bigger than the mustard. In my flesh's weak condition, I'm crying out with all of the strength that I've mustered. I'm feeling flustered. What's even worse is that we met at church in a single's group cluster. My sweet tooth won't allow me to not eat of her custard. So tell me why do I lust her. Why would you make a slab of ribs, and expect me to eat just her? Maybe the comfort of the environment rushed her. I'm trying to shine but I think that I'm beginning to lack my luster. I'm sipping holy water browner than Buster...Rhymes in times like these, I'm just asking can I trust her. Should I stay or retreat like General Custer. God, I think that I love her...This is Cocktails coming from my prayer vigil home cubicle. If something's on your mind, let it off.

EXCUSE ME MISS

Excuse me Miss. I don't mean to be a bother. But I wanted to introduce myself, because when I saw you, I could walk no farther...or further. You seem filled with fervor. And your father probably tells your dates that, "You don't deserve her". But I would tell him that I know you are his twinkling little star, and I would love to observe her. Who wouldn't want to hear the radiance of your voice, because I know that you've heard her. Let me start off by saying that I can't afford Berber. But if looks could kill, they should be booking you for murder. You're killing me softly with your song. And when you think of me, think of long. Long walks, long talks, about what you long for. Because if we know each other then we would get along more. Feeling like we belong together wouldn't be an oblong chore. I feel you to my soul's core. I would keep a smile on your face, because I would hate to be a bore. And I know that you abhor gentlemen approaching you like you are a piece of meat. And I know that every guy wants a piece on the first date after you meet. But I just want to bring you peace from this rat race track meet. You can stop running, because I brought some Epson Salt for your feet. I would treat you so good even your friends would throw salt trying to compete. But I only have eyes for you, and I'm grown, so our actions would be discreet. This Yin Yang connection would make our circle complete, like a platinum CD put on repeat. So, Hi my name is Chris, and it's a pleasure to know you. I can't explain this attraction, but I'd love to show you. You are my Visine, making my vision clearer. Too bad I'm saying this; all to my mirror...This is Cocktails coming from my shy brother home cubicle. Communication is key.

IT'S A NEW YEAR

For my line brother's wedding...

Today is a new year, it's our anniversary. It's a new year. When I met you it was New Year's. You were in the middle of the dance floor amongst your peers. During the cheers and the here's here. During the turning of the century year. God put you here. A diamond shining in the club amongst the coal. You opened my soul like a bottle full of bubb..ly. You were looking so lovely. Who knew that this woman would grow to love me. Not judge me and during arguments not begrudge me. Excuse me Miss, normally I don't do this, but I think that an angel just nudged me. May old acquaintance be forgot, I think not. I think that I want to tie the knot, and give it my best shot. Maybe buy a plot on a city block in a good neighborhood without extra locks. Something with a cool breeze because I heard that you came from a windy spot. Instead of giving you a rock, I'll give you Anita Baker. I'm giving you the best that I've got, baby and maybe. God willing that will be enough, and God willing it won't be so rough. But God will make us tough, just like God made us. And in His trust, is, God's will. And I trust you to be my nurse when I am ill. I trust that when I am drowning, you will be my gills. I trust that when I am hungry, you will be my meals. I trust that in our joint ventures you won't steal. I trust that during our 7-year itch, we'll scratch it and be together still. I'm just keeping it real. Today is a new year, it's our anniversary. It's a new year and together we can face our fears. Listen to each other with new ears, catapult each other to new tiers. Clutch each other when we switch gears. Rear our children and love them dear. Together shed joyful new tears, together stay genuine and sincere. And forever stay near to each other. My mind, body, and soul lover, thank you for loving a brother. Who knew that with a new year I'd discover. A woman who would hover above my world so my life will never be the same. Today is a new year, it's our anniversary. It's a new year, but there's been a change. Today until forever, you have my last name.

YOU INTIMIDATE ME

You intimidate me. My Goddess Queen. It's the oddest thing that you make this artist sing, and freely give of his modest means. My movie star in the hottest scenes. You intimidate me. Because I don't want to mess up. You make me want to clean my mess up. I'm coming clean to fess up. You in my life has been the best luck. For your happiness I would spend the best bucks. We can escalate in Escalades and the best trucks. And any man that disrespects you best duck. Let's tuck, and hideaway. You strip my hide away. I don't want to let you to slip and slide away. I just want to grip your hips and guide you away to my passenger seat for us to ride away. I'll be there by your side like Sade. My sweet Sade…lady. You are my sweetest taboo, and I'm staying true because my heart made me. Maybe these fruitful words will produce babies, and we can give them black names like "Lil' J" and "Mercedes". I'm playing, but this is what I'm saying. When I'm around you I start acting all gay and bashful. When I'm normally real brashful and abrasive, but when I'm in your presence I'm evasive. Because you intimidate me. My Goddess Queen. It's the oddest thing that you make this artist sing, and freely give of his modest means. My movie star in the hottest scenes. You…intimidate…me..and I like it. This is Cocktails coming from my home cubicle of forlorn dreams. Let that person know how you feel.

HERE'S THE PLAN

Here's the plan. Two Candles, Two Place Settings, and baked ziti in the pan. Dreaming of potholders on your shoulders, because you're hot in my hands. Hotter than broken fans. Hotter than black turbans riding across desert sands. Iraq my brain as the flames hit the pot, is that a knock, so to the door Iran. Please understand. I can't wait for our intimate date. Leave room for cake. I don't cake. These cats act fake. When being themselves is all it takes. Come inside, relax lady, and take a break. You're in good hands like AllState. Sit down and sip some wine while I fix your plate. Woman thou art loosed like T.D. Jakes. Let's converse about topics ranging from bad relationship breaks to political debates. Be careful, sometimes I bait with my homemade brownies that I bake. Like you, I have a fetish for chocolate, and with your skin, I can't wait to catch a toothache. Your nickname must be Tony the Tiger, because you're grrrreeaat. Sit by the fire, so I can melt your Frosted Flakes. Your sensuousness is innate, but you keep it caged like an inmate. Our vulnerability is mutual so fling open your gates. How about you, me, and a clean slate. At any rate, I'm willing to give the best that I can. Here's the plan. I got that magic man…This is Cocktails coming from my home blind date cubicle. Start gearing up for Valentine's Day.

I'M JUST A REGULAR GUY

I'm just a regular guy. I don't own anything fly. I can barely afford to fly. My bank account is bone dry. So I'm just asking why. Why are these chicks trying to mack on me? Because I don't think that feel I'm worthy of this high price tag that they're trying to slap on me. They're amazed after a month saying, Girl he doesn't try to slap on me. He's a gentleman, and doesn't try to crap on me. He doesn't put my insecurities back on me. He has use of all of his faculties, and doesn't smother or tackle me. Actually he tickles me, and when I'm in a pickle, he helps me. That's my husband, who else could it be? Could it be that Cocktails is lonely? Or maybe he can't be with one woman only. My deepest fear is that a woman is trying to own me, and change me from my own me. So to open negotiation, they offer to blow me and bone me. You don't even know me. You must think that I'm dumber than Gilligan on the Island Coney. Take your 3 dollar bill elsewhere to spend, you're phony. Trying to bring your friends around to surround me like Sony. Your brain is fried like bologna. And it takes a strong mental to atone me. This grown me needs time with the alone me. But it's hard when different women are trying to Al Capone me and strong arm me. In order to get a man, they would harm me and swarm me. This is alarming. Because I'm not the only heterosexual male in this situation. This is not an instigation, just a few words to highlight this new reversed courting sensation...This is Cocktails coming from my home cubicle of reasonable doubt. I'm not bitter, just cautious.

SHE

(My part of Abyss's poem "She") She is my wait til the midnight hour. She is my Calgon from Shower to Shower. Her sun fuels my solar power. She gives me the strength to bear my soul when I used to be a coward. She stays sweet even when I act sour. I think that I want to pollinate her flower. She provides shade as if the two towers never fell. When I am hanging off the cliff, she is my nails. When life has me locked down, she is my bail. When the going gets tough, I know that she won't bail. I am her LL and she rocks my bells. I rock her when we spoon, kiss and never tell. I love it when my room has the aromatherapy of shower gel smells. She allows me to be the Alpha male. She is attentive when I describe my Alpha tales. She knows why I am called Cocktails. She also knows my first name is Ell..U..N. I would be catching L's if I didn't have you in. She is the conflict resolution to my UN. I know that I have been fighting against it, but you win. Imagine what my life would be like if I knew you back when. If I laid my burdens down would your back bend. She unpacked my baggage when it was packed in. She nourished me back to health when my trust was crack thin. She could be using her powers to mack men. But she spends hours teaching and educating young black men. I could see her on family road trips with our young in the back strapped in. It's amazing this grace that has happened. And above all else, she is just she...This is Cocktails coming from my home cubicle of self growth. Everybody needs a little bit.

I AM WAITING FOR YOU TO RUN

I am waiting for you to run. Everyday I wonder if you are sitting there waiting for me to do something dumb. I know that you have been sitting there saying do something dumb..ey. Slanting your eyes like Gumby. Think of all of the times when we kissed that you gave your gum to me. Trying to make me freeze like you have a gun to me. Look at what you've done with me. Are you going to quit now and be done with me? I just needed to see if you could run with me. That's why it's called "For Starters", because I needed you to run with me. And appetizers are "For Starters", but I need the leftovers to come with me. If you are my cake, I'm even taking the crumbs with me. It's not my intention to make you feel crummy. I haven't loved for a long time, and there is a strange feeling in my tummy. And it's hard for me to "Cher" (share), because I've been a bachelor Sonny. And it 'bees' like that sometimes in order for me to protect my honey. My heart is like money, and I don't want the bank broken. So if you're willing to ride, please accept these nonrefundable tokens. And on relaxing days we can be creative with our loafing with conversation wide open about personal notions. So please don't misconstrue my sarcasm and joking, it's my way of coping with a special someone. It feels too good to be true, and I feel guilty having so much fun. That's why I am waiting for you to run...This is Cocktails coming from my home cubicle of insecurities. We all have them.

I AM WAITING FOR YOU TO COME

I am waiting for you to come. I long to wipe the crust from your eye while your face is partially lit by the waking sun. My heart pitter-patters simultaneously with the rhythm of pitter-patter of feet from our waking son. Do you want some coffee because I just finished making some? Do you want butter on your blueberry muffins because I just finished baking some? Marriage plus years equals our dating sum. I still remember asking if you actively date, and you said, "some". At the time your mating was numb, and you blessed and bestowed me to be the 'someone'. And when men asked you out, you politely replied, "I already have someone." It feels good to rub my ring and know that I have someone. My Lord and My Ring made you 'my precious' hon…ey. Today marks the day that I submitted on one knee. I was the one crying because you knew I didn't have any money. And you allowed me to make the greatest purchase of all. You accepted my heart as collateral, and you never let us fall. And with each new year that has been ushered in, you don't have to call. I recall when we first got married we still had to crawl. Now we've grown to ten years tall, and our love is stronger than day one. Everyday from the waking of the sun until the day is done, I won't just settle for anyone. I know that God will send me the one. That's why I'm still waiting for you to come…This is Cocktails coming from my Valentine's forlorn home cubicle. Love is a beautiful thang.

IT'S NOT FAIR

It's not fair to her. I'm not giving enough care to her. I see she's suffocating and I'm not getting enough air to her. She's giving her all, and I'm not giving my share to her. I'm not taking any risks, and everything is a dare to her. She doesn't know that my man armor won't allow me to be bare to her. I can't show my feelings and be scared to her. And the fear of not knowing is beginning to tear at her. Because she wants 'my company', but doesn't know if I'll give my chair to her. We are at the point of breaking up or getting married to her. But I don't know if I'm prepared for her. To wake up everyday and have to stare at her. I want it to be a loving look instead of a glare at her. And it's not like I want to split hairs with her. I want to climb the stairs with her. But my poker face won't show my hand, so she can see it's one pair with her. I'm an endangered species so my mannerisms are rare to her. My habitat is a lion's lair to her. But her 'whip' appeal is taming and no other lionesses compare to her. And 'my pride' has to be tamed so I can have a career with her. Despite of how things appear to her. I've enjoyed spending these years with her. I want the same things that she holds dear to her. But spoken words couldn't articulate my stance and make it clear to her. That's why it's not fair to her...This is Cocktails coming from my home cubicle of machoness (if that's a word). Ladies don't give up on us, we have issues sometimes too.

GROWTH

Growth. I've seen it in us both. Equally yoked, unlike the parasite and the host. Even though both of us have been burned like toast. Feeding each other rope to see which one will be the first to make a noose and choke. But we hung loose, so we wouldn't be at each other's throat. Building a foundation on trustful hope instead of lustful strokes. Now my life is sweeter, because I started using your soap. You were able to get through my a$$hole approach, and appreciate my corny jokes. You saw my wealth, even though my bank account read "broke". You even got some cool folks. Apprehensive to see if you are the real thing like Coke. Outkasted trying to find my prototype, singing Tupac hymns of the realest thing I ever wrote. Hard to sing harmony, because most of these chicks were hollering at me in tone deaf notes. Disguising themselves in makeup coats, and bible quotes. My friends went from, "Cocktails settle? Nope." To, "I don't mean to mettle and poke, but don't be a dope." I've been letting it marinate and soak. Maybe I could let down my bridge and let you cross the moat...This is Cocktails coming from my home cubicle of growth. It's scary, but necessary.

MY VISION

My vision was slightly slanted. But you straightened me up, and taught me how to not take things for granted. Granted, we couldn't have known it would work out this well even if we planned it. But we believed in Black Thought and kept our Roots planted. Before, I would have a fire escape route if I smelled smoke, even if I was the one that fanned it. But you kept me in check without me feeling that I was being reprimanded. And that balance led to trust that you won't be underhanded. If they hate then let them hate because they don't understand it. They are just mad because you are happy and they can't stand it. Maybe one day we can be at the same altar where our parents standed (stood). And outside influences can't alter our ideas because our conversations have been candid. People isolate themselves, then cry for help when they realize that they're stranded. That's why over half of these unions end up disbanded. Because they tackle problems individually, and don't realize, "We can get through this banded." Call me chauvinistic, but brothers don't feel like the head, because they don't command it. We concentrate on finding a 10 instead of following the 10 Commandments. But a those come a dime a dozen and commercialism has made them outlandish. With age and wisdom it dulls the senses of ego and being mannish. True I'm not completely out the wilderness, but I've learned to maintain and manage. Maybe my wounds have healed, I'm just scared to take off the bandage...This is Cocktails coming from my home cubicle of turning a New Year's Leaf. Who told you that you were naked?

JIGSAW PUZZLE

We are the outside borders of a jigsaw puzzle. Trying to piece together our personal traits like attractiveness to desire, or strength to muscle. You said you would stand by me like a gang war tussle. You pulled my calmness out, even during the hustle and bustle. How we got our pieces to fit, with the notion I still wrestle. You were the smooth edges, and I was the abstract rebel. You watched me lay on my bed of rocks, and still considered them pebbles. And you remained there to nurse the sores when I said ouch. Even when my rocks were jagged, you allowed me to sleep on your couch. We used to lie on that same couch and you would tell me about your insecurities with your kangaroo pouch. But I told you baby I am the Marlboro man with a tobacco pouch, rolling Joe Camels smoking across the desert sand. Trying to find your oasis because I stay Kool. And I stay Kalm. Calm like the palm tree during winter in the eye of a hurricane storm. Patience allows this jigsaw relationship to take form. Wonder Twins activate in the form of a heart. That is the complete picture on the puzzle box, but the borders are where we start. What God has pieced together, let no man break apart…This is Cocktails from my home cubicle of Valentine's wishes. Enjoy your relationships.

SWEET THANG

Sweet Thang...Honey suckle, making my knees buckle, feathers ruffle, exposing my peacock stance. Make me do that mating dance. Hypnotic beauty leaving me in a trance at the first glance. Tongue out, quickened breath, heavy pants. Talk to her, no, I can't. Caramel Chewy, Honey Dewey melons. Scared of pursuing this mission and failing. Sweat dripping. I'm tripping. Thinking about brown skin up against my brown skin. Black berry molasses melanin. Bath and Body Works. I'm smelling, keep inhaling. Mental thoughts derailing into the gutter. Her? Butter...no Parkay. What can I say to make her sway my way. Look happy, but not gay. Smile don't let your eyes stray. We connect, she smiles and mouth it's okay. Without hesitation I start my presentation, "Hey"....This is Cocktails coming from my cubicle dating game.

SPRING CONFESSIONS

Couples copulate and are cut off from cooperative coalition concerning constant consonants creating candid conversation. Never deserving degradation her elation is equivalent to constipation when she can sense bullsh*t in the negotiation. Your game is tailored off of play station instead of trying to instill palpitations and sensations from a mental congregation. Can the church say Amen while a grin is indented in her chin. Since the negotiation is a game at least I can try to win. How can I skip what is your name, and go straight to, where you been? However my memory of pretty faces is a recycle bin, as they recycle Bin Ladens and Saddaam Husseins. All I wanted was something constant, because it's been a lot of them, and my opening is "Say damn, are you sane?" I want you to stay the same. I stay plain because me being shiny would change our aim. I'd rather be Dick Tracey and you be my dame. Me Tarzan, You Jane. My Appollonia in Purple Rain. There is no joy in your pain. There would be no hyphen in our last name. We would outlast fame. And I want to live forever engrained in your brain…This is Cocktails coming from my home cubicle of spring confessions. Be single by choice.

I WANT YOU TO KNOW WHAT LOVE IS

I want to know what love is. I want you to show me, hold me, mold me. I want you to be everything that my heart has told me. Stay in my presence never leave me lonely. Let me hold you every night, just you only. Every day I awaken I long to hear your voice, melodically flowing from your soft red lips. My soul mate that has me made monogamous by choice. I drink in your being longing for another sip, of your fine wine, girl you're so fine. Not only in body, but a beautiful soul. Personality ageless, I know we'll stand the test of time. Joined together at the hip, dwelling until we're old. Love can't be sold, nor can it be bought. Stand with me through the thick and thin. I can't describe this feeling, nor can it be taught. Intoxicated with your grace, faithful until the end. Spend eternity with me as we sit in heaven looking down. At our grandchildren and their children that we have raised. Sitting with Jesus that has blessed us with our crowns. Sending guardian angels to protect them in their days. Give me this honor to have and to hold, devote my love to protect and respect you for the rest of my life. You are my precious rose and peaceful dove. So this day I ask you to be my wife. I Love you...(Long sigh) Unfortunately, I have no one to tell this to, so I'll just cry in my pillow for Valentine's Day. This is Cocktails singing sonnets from my cubicle gift basket.

Chapter 2
Drink 2

The Real Thoughts

Brain Candy

Ingredients

1 1/2 oz Alize, 1 oz Malibu Rum, 1 part Orange Juice, 1 part Pineapple Juice, 1 splash Grenadine, 1 splash Ginger Ale

Mixing Instructions

Shake alcohols and juices. Add to glass with ice. Pour Grenadine and Ginger Ale on top. Garnish with Cherry and Orange Wheel.

Elevators

(To the tune of "Elevators" by Outkast) One for the money, yes
sir, two for the show. A couple of years ago on the east side,
Candler Rd, was the start of something good. When me and Abyss
rode the Taurus through the hood. Just trying to find that hook up,
everyday we looked up at the screen, struggling in corporate
America trying to make that cream, off the man. Here's the plan,
on Microsoft Word, printing poems out, hitting open mics to be
heard. Getting emails, surfing the web, trying to find our niche off in
the spot, spot off in the niche. Hoping we don't get caught. Doing
the hole in the wall clubs, this here must stop, like freeze, we making
the crowd move, but still have thin cheese, and that's a no no… A
one two, a one two, dope poets in the city yes they call us. Went
from reading on paper to flawless. Putting the south up on the map
by traveling and entertaining. We said forget all that playing, they
paying. We staying helping locals with our vocals up in the commu-
nity, Live Poets keeps it real, trying to form our own industry. Over
15,000 emails to this date, people don't take it lightly. 2006 is
going to be that year that all of the promoters start to invite we, to
your town. (sing the hook) Me and you. Yo momma and yo
cousin too. Need to come to our shows. Live Poets has food for
the soul…This is Cocktails coming from my home studio cubicle.
We trying to move up like Elevators.

Controversial Views

People think that I have controversial views. I like to think of it as conversational news. I provide the clues, and have people figure it out by using their own tools. Who made up your ethical set of rules? I follow my instinct and experience from paying my dues. While most people are playing ESPN office pools, I'm in the coal mine searching for rare jewels. Nay Sayers get worked up like mules, and think that my honesty is cruel. When was the last time someone challenged you to a duel? Better to make them think that you are a fool when your mouth is closed; because when you open it your views of reality are exposed. I write this for the youth that think their existence hinges on designer clothes and bankrolls. I write this for the adults that hop on bandwagons and people choice polls. I mean no harm when I cajole, but don't cringe when the truth is told. God made his people to be bold. He broke the mold, and people try to clone someone else, so the image can be resold. If this is the Matrix, then we definitely need to reload. In close, take an honest inventory within and see if you are reaching your goals. If you have no foundation then your structure will topple whenever the wind blows. Don't rely on what men know and follow your heart and soul.

Punch Lines

I don't write punch lines to punch dimes. I punch rhymes to punch minds. I punch the blind in the eye hard to make them see that when they punch time cards, there is no security, ask the unemployed in the lunch line. We starving artists don't have money to crunch numbers, so we crunch lines. It's Game Time. Waiting for our big break in Game 7 to take the shot in crunch time. We write hot flows that are liquid like soup in thermoses at lunchtime. We are "mm mm good" like Campbell's and crackers, and I munch mine. I stay up at night during hunch time creating ideas bigger than the Brady Bunch at prime time. The so-called underground that is mainstream is still walking a fine line. These commercials by design make my "cute little poetry thing" prices decline, because they want the talent, but claim that they don't have any money in the bottom line. We started this thing from the bottom with lines, and most cats want to hop in the glamour and never experience the grime. But I love the true grit and smell from microphone spit on these different poetry pipelines. I write this for the youth that write rhymes during study hall and serving in school suspension time. It's pay attention time. I feel like a hot Corona, because I see the light, but have no lime. They say everything comes in time, and I'm like a mime waiting for God to send me a sign. Maybe He's taking his time, because my tithes are behind. It's hard to break these material shackles that bind. But I'll stay on the grind until my lifeline meets its deadline. Because the heart's ink never runs out of lines...This is Cocktails coming from my home entertainment center cubicle. Never give up.

Friend or Foe

Halt! Who goes there? Friend or Foe. Nowadays I just don't know. I ask God what's it all foe. He tells me that I need to read His infoe. It's the same old story we've all heard befoe. Foe Horsemen galloping across the sky. One year ago, there wasn't a dry eye in NY. Others were too stunned to cry. With our wake up call anniversary on the horizon, I find these political acts surprising. Wasn't it just one year ago that we had this uprising? Critics say that a copy cat attack is enticing. Since the president needs advising, someone tell him to stop mising. I'm surmising that we need some spiritual Visine. Get the red out that bled out when the firemen couldn't get out. When the light was shed out, leaving a dark cloud, muffling the screams out loud. You still toting a flag acting proud? Forty years ago we were forming rally crowds, because we weren't allowed...watch who you befriend, befoe you let them in your front door. This is Cocktails coming from my cubicle watchtower.

Apologies

I don't apologize for what I write. Until they apologize for our plight. And even then that still doesn't make it right. Because they have instilled fright. Now I have to instill esteem before I can instill fight. We have the tallest achievements, but won't dunk because we are ashamed of our height. We've been neutered to be all bark and no bite. And the shades we wear are to hide sorrow instead of it being because our future is so bright. After shows people come up to me and tell me, "You are so right". Then go home and instead of helping the cause, stay out of sight. Sword of Omens give me sight beyond sight. Sores of old men give me insight from hind sight. Our situation has always been tight. But we still manage to expand with a tightened up waistband. We have Indian in our family, but if it hadn't been stolen by the man, would we still waste land? Maybe we hid our talents in burial grounds, and Elvis dug them up while he was shooting his movies and took them to Graceland. It was intended for people of color to be the finest race to grace man. Why do you think people of different races tan? Because it's innate when all different faces' roots are African. But they don't want to hear that so they divided us with a hyphen and added American. I wish I could have been in the meetings when the forefathers of this nation were devising this apparent plan. Because whatever was said has transferred and engrained into our head. And whoever went against the law of the land no matter what status ended up dead. For years the enemy has been sleeping in our bed. So when we are bred, we take orders lying down, because that's how we are fed. Now ignorance has spread because what we haven't tried we dread. And tears are being shed from not trying and right now it looks like were dying to be led…This is Cocktails coming from my home cubicle of community activism. We have everything we need; we just have to combine our resources.

Sticks and Stones

Sticks and stones may break your bones, but words pierce the soul. Would you let someone pierce your hand, then come back and show them the holes? Is the end justified by the means if you reach your goal? God deals us hands to either play out or fold. Made in his mold is the greatest biblical story ever told. Is that why the great leaders of our society never make it to being old? Because they tried to do the righteous thing and was shot down by scoffs and scolds. Now we keep the positive people underground like a mole. People want the diamonds without purchasing the coal. There is no 'I' in Team, but everybody wants the starring role. Would God punch your name when he goes to the polls? I learned a long time ago, either you get rolled over or you're the one that rolls. What did you put on your resolutions scroll?...This is Cocktails coming from my home recovery station (I was the New Year's Baby :-)

I'm Not Disgruntled...I'm Perturbed

I'm not disgruntled. It's just that my emotions are tightly bundled. I'm focused man, but America's vision is tunneled. It's more than oil that's being funneled, they are draining our brains. Taking away morals and replacing it with pain. Equating sex, drugs, and being controversial to obtaining fame. Reality shows aren't displaying the reality of being plain. We didn't act like coons and buffoons on "College Hill" and still were off the chain. Where are my young people willing to go against the grain. Because they have you where they want you, and assign you the blame. While they are writing history, you will be referred to as a stain. Because they feed you with bullsh!t, and then look at you with disdain when you act out in Hip Hop's name. This isn't why Hip Hop came. But how can you tell someone to get crunk, then wonder why they don't act tame. Teach them to act ignorant or else they are lame. Tell them life ain't nothing but cars, clothes, and a naked dame. Pump them up with Riddlin for ADD, and then classify them as Special Ed and insane. When I talk to them, I see that they are thirsting for the Lord to make it rain. Wild horses are dragging them away, and no one will pull the reigns. So they find comfort in Ecstasy and Mary Jane. Because their parents are doing it too, and they want to feel the same. Peer Pressure has them with no driver's license living in the fast lane. Looking for the next popular craze to pump through their veins. We took spirituality out of their life curriculum, maybe we need to put it back in the main...This is Cocktails coming from my home cubicle of unadulterated listening. When I was a child, I spoke as a child...

Problems

They say if you are not part of the solution, you're part of the
problem. Well my part of the problem is that I've been imparting
my problems in my efforts to solve them. I try to work it out
myself, so people, I don't have to involve them. Because I don't
want to feel like I'm using them and being an intrusion. Actually, the
reality is that they need inclusion. And since I've been giving you
part of my problems, here's part of the solution. Spread positivity
and community like pollution. Practice respectful dialogue to avoid
confusion. If you have resources, use them. I said use them, not
abuse them. Laugh if you find something amusing. Live is already
bruising. So, instead of taking blows, beat on negativity until it has
contusions. If someone is feeling down, boost them. Entrepreneur-
ial literature, peruse them. Honesty and ethical practices, induce
them. It's elementary my dear Watson, the little things, deduce
them. Don't let the big things serve as distractions. Do what you
love with passion. Face fears head on and attack them. If you
know someone is right, then back them. When making big deci-
sions, use ration. Take responsibility and have accountability
instead of passing. Then can we see the momentum of believers
amassing. Part of the solution to start healing is positive interaction.

Economics

I've been looking for stock tips to keep afloat my income tax ship because Bush's economic stimulus plan is bullsh!t, and he finally got the chance to push it. But I'm not Salt and Pepper and the stress is starting to pepper my hair with salt. Uncle Sam's finger keeps pointing at me saying, "It's your fault". The government is making me hustle illegally, and I'm trying not to get caught. But how can I take a test for a subject in which I've never been taught. America is the greatest piece of property that was never bought. Yet it has brought for so much wealth with no overhead. We went from gunpowder in muskets to bombs flying over our heads. Call us McDonalds with over one million dead. They keep giving me media sleeping pills to help me lie in this bed. But it's hard to rest your head when the mattress is made of nails. We still blaming that ship made of sails, and then say a Willie Lynch letter predestined us to fail. Instead of savings, we keep saving for bail. BET keeps black mailing the black male so if the MTV Crib isn't for sale we can move in the big house full of cells. With no father, these kids are living like garbage pails. Play station has them impaled, desensitized, and cold blooded until their face is pale. I really wish our races could gel.

Reasons for Writing

Do I write what I think, or do I write what I think people want me to write. I write from insight, or whatever is in sight. But if I write what I really think then a riot would incite…inside. A lot of my opinions I hide because my politically correct side tells me to lie. Actually I don't lie. I just see queer behavior with a straight eye. We categorize straight behavior and pass queer notions by. But truth be told, both lives still encompass straight lies, and we exhale sighs laced with hate and despise. Deez spies cry wolf and follow like sheep to their own demise. They come in the name of the Lord, but yell Judas denies. And I can't deny the existence of alternative lives, nor do I try to hate, because we still have half these guys that are straight not pulling their weight. So who am I to say how to get your life straight, or how to achieve your life fate? I still feel like I started my life purpose late, and some people are still looking for life to serve their plate. But I do believe how you live your life determines how He serves your fate. And this poem is probably going to receive great debate, but this is reality that David Blaine can't even escape. And crimes of hate can't turn into hope, when there are so many goats to be made scape. Our morals have hit bottom and are beginning to scrape, and we can't rest on our laurels because of the blows that the foundation is beginning to take. You can't have bittersweet ingredients and still try to bake some-thing fake, and get mad when other people don't want to eat your cake. Every body made up their own set of religious rules of how to reach Heaven's Gate. Don't be surprised when we all get up there, and the Lord has a sign posted "Out for Lunch, Be Back in Eternity". How long would you wait…this is Cocktails coming from my home cubicle of theological rhetoric. Stop worrying about what the next person is doing, and concentrate on self.

Giving Up

Sometimes I just want to throw in the towel. Because it's harder
for my consonants to connect when I'm broke and can't buy a
vowel. I feel like no one gives a hoot when I impart my wisdom
like the owl. And this pressure is starting to make me scowl. A hit
dog will holla so listen to this howl. I talk a lot of shit but can't get it
together like loose bowels. My mental constipation keeps me
uptight like Colin Powell. And this procrastination has all of my
sentences starting with, "Tomorrow I'll". In the meanwhile my
unpaid bills are starting to pile. And my diet consists of ramen
noodles that taste like fowl. Lord, I'm banging hard in the paint for
rebounds, and I'm still not getting the foul. What's the point if tax
day comes; I have no income to file. These words are my debt to
society waiting for some equity to compile. And the pain is making
me grimace, but people think it's a smile. If image is nothing, why
does everyone follow the same style? My thirst is everything, and
everything tastes mild. I'm on my own, God Bless this child. My
momma's birthday is coming and I still haven't walked down the
aisle. Because I have no time for dating or to be beguiled. Their
disgust for my lack of attention gives them the loose neck like a
cowl. I want to have a queen to be, but they have ulterior motives
when they bow. I pray that I don't have ulterior motives when I
take my vows. Because I have seen too many P.O.W's (Prisoners
of Weddings). I want me and my mate to be pals, instead of her
taking the maximum amount of alimony allowed. Maybe you can't
hear my thoughts so allow me to read this out loud. Protect me as I
put my thoughts in front of a crowd. Keep me grounded, because I
can't see if my head is in the clouds. I confess this with my mouth.
I Need You Now.

Chapter 3
Drink 3

Spiritual

Fallen Angel

Ingredients

1 1/2 oz Gin, 1/2 Tsp White Creme de Menthe, Juice of 1/2 Lemon, 1 dash Bitters, 1 Cherry

Mixing Instructions

Shake al ingredients (except cherry) with ice and strain into a cocktail glass. Top with the cherry and serve.

Faith

Faith is the substance of things hoped for. Based on my substance it seems that my faith should have hoped for more. This isn't what I hoped for Lord. The train seemed beautiful when I hopped on board. But I didn't know that it was going to hop the tracks. Take the path less traveled picking up underground railroad blacks. That don't know they are free, even when presented with the facts. I'm trying to pave the road, but my concrete has cracks. From constant stress, pressure, and spiritual attacks. The burden is starting to put a strain on my back. And sometimes it feels like I'm jumping butt naked into a pool of thumbtacks. It hurts. Is this what it takes to carve your place in history before the Hearse? What's worse is I haven't been attending much church. I know that it's my spiritual vitamin, but I need an at home nurse. To nurture my blessing so it won't relapse into a curse. I'm trying to figure out a formula that works. My writing comes out in spurts and blurts. How can I be a guidance counselor, if I'm the one going beserk? Leading people through the wilderness, knowing that evil lurks. Giving free advice, because they don't believe in my worth. But they believe in man made hell on earth. We are all looking for salvation, how did I become the one leading the search? I planted my faith of the mustard seed. Lord, please fertilize my dirt

Hear O Lord

Hear O Lord when I cry with my voice. Have mercy on me. Fill my vessel so the words that I utter (udder) will have people nursing on me. Because right now it feels like vampires are thirsting on me. These people with puffed up pride trying to be stars are bursting on me. It seems like individuals who's sole intentions are messing over someone are rehearsing on me. I'm trying to be a good man with a soft nest, but pigeons and chicken heads keep perching on me. Fake thugs keep lurking on me. Holier than thou Christians are churching on me. Bill Collectors and credit reports are putting a hurting on me. I know that you have been working with me. I thought that we were committed, but are you still flirting with me? It's been somewhat disconcerting to me. What I believe to be right is failing, and it's becoming deterring to me. I'm beginning to entertain the negative thoughts that have been occurring to me. It feels like the stories about people with wasted potential and talent are referring to me. Right now nothing seems certain to me. White people keep talking urban to me. Instead of curtain calls, the devil is saying it's curtains for me. My fight club doesn't even have a Tyler Durden for me. I'm being treated like I'm walking through an airport with a turban on me. I've been wearing do-rag headwrap bandages because the stress has my head hurting, and it's becoming disturbing to me. I rebuke this spirit of despair that has been stirring in me. Lord, hear my voice and have mercy on me. I'm placing my burdens at your feet.

I Can't Take a Day Off

My intensity won't let me take a day off. Because I'm trying to stay in your head like Stay Soft. I have to push my marketing scheme harder, because the media has our conscious way off. We buy lottery tickets looking for the big pay off. And kids sit around the house like they're laid off. While there are people under the rubble in Iran that still lay lost. God's athletes are in the midst of the playoffs, and we can't take a play off. The devil has an all out blitz, and I'm trying not to get burned. I'm at the line trying to call an audible, and make sure my voice is audible, because I'm concerned. I've been asking for my prayers to be confirmed. Because the devil is in my left ear and God is in my right, and images are becoming hard to discern. My circumstantial evidence alone is enough to convict me when the court is adjourned. But life is a journey, and Cochran is mortal. So I'll take Jesus as my attorney. And he gave me one more chance with a mistrial. I know I'm blessed because the devil advised me to miss my trial. My probation period was filled with tribulations and trials. And libation periods had me filled with lust and beguile. I found myself praying to the porcelain god, telling the people outside that I would be a while. Now I find myself praying and talking about God, telling incoming calls that I would be a while. It's hard for peers to fathom change when you used to be wild. That doesn't mean that I've turned mild. It just means that I have unfinished business, and it's a big pile. Thank you Lord, because doing your work gives me a big smile…This is Cocktails coming from my home cubicle inbox. Faith without works is dead.

Never Block Your Blessings

Never block your blessings. Faith and Trust means that I have to unlearn what I have learned, and that is the hardest lesson. These multiple choices in life keep me guessing. That's why I stay in late night smoke filled sessions. Trying to invoke the spirit of keep on pressing instead of stressing about making lasting first impressions. Hopefully God doesn't find flaws in my system at first inspection. But my tithes weren't enough to cover my warranty on my soul's protection. I'm just trying to get my name on the ballot, so I can participate in the election. But Darwin got these human mammals being savage for natural selection. You can tame the wildest beast with affection. But I'm not plastic man, and I can't tell how far my love is stretching. I feel like I have a glass house, and the devil gave his dogs sticks and stones for fetching. And he throws them at my house with unwarranted aggression, hoping that I might not tell my Dad in confession. But Dad turns the sticks into my number 2 pencils for testing. With whom do you think your messing? Never block your blessings. Faith and Trust truly are the hardest lessons…This is Cocktails coming from my home sweat shop. Never give up on your goals.

God Is Good All The Time

God is good all the time, and all the time God is good. But why is it that we don't do what we should, and then claim that God's plan is misunderstood? Actually God's plan is very clear, and we take random acts to proclaim that the end is near. But His end is infinite, and He just wants to put a voice in our ear, and whisper understanding, but what we don't understand we fear. That's a factor because even the believers don't sound sincere, and to think that your pressure is only from your peer. But peer into the mind of a club full of tears because they feel pressure from being pressed against a door, or the pressure of feet from being pinned to the floor. Even an atheist will call for God to his soul's core, and pray for the waves hitting the shore to extinguish the fire causing eternal sores. Burning the same flesh that we wrestle against, that paid for religion for hire. Watching the CNN wire that the space shuttle expired, and through pain, all of a sudden people become inspired. You are Blessed and Highly Favored, how can you be tired…This is Cocktails coming from my home cubicle of Blessings. Don't take these signs in the world lightly. Keep positive, don't buy into the negativity.

Moving Forward

God, thank you for a new year. Thank you for keeping me around positive peers and shedding joyful tears. Thank you for putting my words and voice on people's ears. Thank you for helping me face my fears. Thank you for allowing me to speak to the people that will hear. Thank you for advancing our movement from the rear and making our vision clear. Hopefully they will hold these truths dear. Even in being sincere, people have selective memories like scrap-books, because they scrapped their books, and replaced it with pseudo good looks and BS hooks. Now our queens are being pimped by rooks, and half of these women can't cook. And half of these suburb kids want to be crooks. If we were still in the 50's and 60's would we have what it took, when we were against the odds and forsook. Half of these R & B soft males would be shook, and scared to look out the window at a burning cross. So they ice out their cross to please their Klan boss, even if it means taking a financial loss. God help me to walk through the valley of shadows because your sheep are lost. And half of these prophets and preachers are false. I'll keep pressing onward, because on my back I feel salt. I'll keep learning, because I have to unlearn what I was taught. I know that your Son's dying wasn't for naught

I Am The One

I am God. All three in one. You use my name and throw it around
for fun. Then get serious when conflict comes. Close your mouth
and open your eardrums. Oh, what a tangled web we've spun.
When people pray to me and then pick up guns. Rape little boys
and give advice to nuns. Treat people unequal and show favoritism
to some. Worship false men and take the poor's crumbs. Taint my
pure air that you breathe in your lungs. You must not trust me or
think I'm dumb. Take prayer out of schools and change the way
that creation begun. This situation is getting bigger than Pun. While
singing the Lord's Prayer, half of you hum. Consecrate your body
with drugs and rum, then wonder where the pestilence and disease
comes from. Invite me into your heart, because right now
it's numb. I have always been there, I even sent my Son. I show
you my face, but instead you run. And you have the nerve to
wonder why you are not on my scroll when your days are done? I
AM THE ONE...

Lead Me

Lead Me. Lead me Lord, Lead Me. Right now we need Thee. I am hungry, feed me. I know it's hard to believe me because of all the times I've tried to deceive Thee. I planted my mustard seed to grow, weed me. In your court, no contest, is what my plead would be. When I felt trapped you freed me. I know it took a movie to finally grieve He. But they still charged us a fee, and 300 million later made it a need to see. But does any of the proceeds go back to the community? It needs to be. You said you have many mansions, deed me. This industry is trying to bleed me. This is "My Sacrifice", Creed Me. Because even the Winans are whining, what happened to Bebe and Cece. "What's Happening" to the world is like a "Rerun", and I can't get you on the line because of "DeeDee". Right now I feel like the devil is going hee-hee. Laughing because he's spraying society with his AK, and we're shooting bee-bees. Lord I know that we have cannons but your soldiers are scared to grab their balls unless they say it on a CD. And the current is DC to electrify current society back to BC. We think that we're so rich without You in "AD", that we bought a vowel and added an "I" in the middle to keep the motherland unhealthy. I see people living off the famine of the land getting wealthy. I am but one man waiting for you to reveal your divine plan. Please Help ME...This is Cocktails coming from my home cubicle of Eyes Wide Shut. Don't you see what's happening?

We are Praying To You

These multitudes of religion are all trying to pray to You. We just think that its a different God we're praying to. I don't know what to say to You. I'm on the Highway to Heaven trying to wave hey to You, and hopefully I can still behave too. We think that it's a two way street, but it's only one way to You. So when I die, I want my one way too. I know that right now the world looks in disarray to You. But I'm painting a big enough sign that says "This Way Too". I'm sorry that I had to present it this way to You. But the devil's signs are even bigger saying "THIS WAY TOO!!". And his worshipers get at You this way too. And he has double agents that insist it's the way too. I am shocked and appalled that man would act this way to You. I'm the next door neighborhood kid wishing that I could stay with You. I'm knocking on the gate saying can I play too? What if instead of us saying, "Can I hit that", we said, "Can I pray too?". So we know that when we exhale our breath is on its way to you. Which is ironic, because our breathing way is through you. Just like our grieving way is through you. You birth us, and we forget that our leaving way is through You. And it's only when we're about to leave that we start agreeing with You. We want the marriage without being with You. But when we divorce, we miss seeing You. We want to be pleased, but miss pleasing You. And still want You to be appeasing too. Hopefully, when I leave this earth you'll have a reason to...this is Cocktails coming from my home cubicle of Faith based writing. The heart never runs out of ink.

Forgive Me Father

Forgive me Father, for I have sinned. It's been two weeks since my last confession. I know that I shouldn't call on your name only when I need a blessing, but see it's this recession. And the bill collectors keep calling and stressing. I don't know if the patience of Job will give me the same lesson. And lately it seems that the answers don't match the questions. These trials of life are testing me, and all I want is my small niche in the entertainment industry. All I see are these street teams like infantries, and half of these shows don't interest me. I would hate to think that my shows are along the same lines because it would incense me. I'm just trying to give back the talents that you chose to invest in me. I feel like a lot of people want to divest me, and how good could my best be. I've been cranky because I haven't been getting a lot of rest see, and I'm scared that if I sleep then someone is going to creep me. These creeps be acting like pseudostars hanging out at the bar, telling me how I'm going to go far. However, I can't recant because I barely have gas in my car. Last week I emptied out my change jar, filled up at the station and bought a snickers bar. I feel like I haven't been going anywhere for a while, and it's getting harder to smile. Were you the metaphor for walking the Green Mile? Right now, it seems that spirituality is out of style. So I'll just end this prayer on knee mail by saying please don't let me fail. In You Do I Excel. As I press the send button, just know that "You've Got Mail". This is Cocktails coming from my home cubicle confession booth. We fall down, but we get up.

Ghetto Superstar

I'd rather be a superstar in the community, than in the industry. Because at least then they would respect me, instead of constantly inspect me. When I leave this earth put "Love Saves" in my eulogy. That goes for the people that approve of me to the people that used me. My peers tell me that I'm not the man that I used to be. I tell them thank you because the Lord's been using me. The devil's mad because He keeps choosing me, even after Satan was misusing me. All these years God keeps bruising me to keep from losing me. I don't want to hit the battlefield and the angels start booing me. I can't fight the warrior spirit that has been brewing in me. Sometimes I wonder what He is doing in me. Is this a spiritual civil war that has been ensuing in me? I'm fighting to win back me, so this is my win back plea. I've been weaning myself from Gin, Jack, and growing seeds. I know that you have been growing seeds conducive to my glowing good deeds. But BET keeps showing these kids pseudo hood needs. And these parents are giving them pseudo good seeds, because they were raised off of no wood paddles and weed. And we are desensitized, because it's nothing to see the next man bleed. I'm so confused, that I'm reading the Holy Quran, holding rosary beads. Praying that the atheists aren't right, because right now they are the first to feed. I keep downing wine and crackers looking for another T.D. Jakes book to read. You said you would supply all of my needs. Right now I need you indeed. Because the devil has the world on lock, and I'm on my cellblock looking for the skeleton key…this is Cocktails coming from my home cubicle of redemption songs. Get a personal rapport with God, and cut the middleman out.

My Soul

My soul is aching, on the edge of breaking. These words are history in the making. I asked God to help me bare my soul, and sometimes it still feels like I'm faking. We ask for redemption and claim our heart is here for the taking, but that sounds good when we know that one day our life will be taken. In the meanwhile our actions are impenitent because we say that God was taking too long. Your call to the throne fizzled out by the end of the gospel song. We all know right from wrong. That's why I write the gospel to purge my wrongs. We finally got our rights and are using them all wrong. Now they are passing bills to reduce our rights and ignorance veils us from their wrongs. People march in the name of King, but don't know the words of "We Shall Overcome" unless P. Diddy remixes the song. Why can't we all just get along? I'll tell you why. Our black leaders are gone, and no one has the balls to step up and speak out against injustices and wrongs. We forward Jesus emails and racial inequality petitions from our comfort zone…at home. The Klan no longer has to throw fire bombs through the window to tell you to be gone, because the men are riding on chrome, out on the roam. While the women are left alone burning aromatherapy candles trying to act like they are cool being on their own. How do we tell these kids to act their age when everything around them is grown? This old soul is starting to moan…This is Cocktails coming from my home cubicle of "I Have a Dream" soul searching. Are you really honoring King's memory by your actions?

Chapter 4
Drink 4

Observations

Reality Twist

Ingredients

1 1/4 oz Amaretto, 1/4 oz Blue Curacao

Mixing Instructions

Fill shot glass full of mostly Amaretto, then carefully
pour Blue Curacao into the middle of the shot glass to
create the "blue twist" down the middle. Looks very
cool if done right.

As I Observed Her

Her jeans were lo cut. But she got offended every time a brother passed by and stared at her butt. And her provocative dress provoked men to address her with the sole intention to cut. I observed this while undressing her with my eyes, laying low in the cut. She was flirtatious but far from a slut. She was comfortable with the attention, so much so, that the free dates she received has caused her to develop a slow gut. But she was uncomfortable with men's ill intentions, so much so, that she was starting to hate their guts. So most of her courting periods had to end abrupt. And I sat there viewing her in a new sorting period and by her demeanor she was having bad luck. I could tell by her attractiveness that most of her life she passed the buck. Because she hasn't had to take responsibility for her actions, but it seemed that her time was almost up. She knew her worth once, but it seems that her esteem was slowly becoming bankrupt. So she stuffed her waist into denim seams and a lo cut shirt with her breasts pushed up. And acted surprised every time the next man pushed up. However she knew that her window of opportunity was about to shut. Eventually, she wouldn't be able to use her body as a crutch. And her fear is that when her curves disappeared men wouldn't interrupt as much. Sadly, like drugs, attention was her rush. Now she's in a rush to find her Prince Charming that could see past his lust. Someone that could wake up and see her with eye crust. Someone that she could still laugh and joke with even when they were old as dust. She knew that soon men's applause of her would slowly hush. So she hung out until last call and the doors were about to shut, turning down offers from drunk nuts. Because she knew she had more to offer, but feared she didn't have enough. So she sat there with cracks in her soul, with her crack exposed from jeans that were lo cut. It's rough trying to hold it together...in the club. This is Cocktails coming from my home cubicle of six minute dating. Know yourself before you meet someone else.

58

It's The Little Things That Count

I listen to women when they say it's the little things. What delight a simple gesture brings instead of being mean. However, it's been overshadowed by the ladies' disgruntled screams because our brothers are scared to be kings. So they think that to get the bling they have to immediately do the wild thing. You are the object in every man's dreams. The problem it seems is that you do not hold your sexuality in high self esteem. And don't realize that the sunlight beams from your crotch. But it sits in bars looking for stars and after he buys you a scotch, you turn into another notch...in his belt. You need some help. A hit dog will holler and I hear a lot of yelps. A lot of women don't have knowledge of self. They search for the brother with the most wealth, and end up being another trophy on the shelf. And I'm sad to say that the men let it happen. We disrespect our queens and want our surroundings to be like video scenes, and we ain't even rapping. Half of these cats have never heard skin slapping. Trying to be fake pimps and keep their mates in check by slapping. What ever happened to conversation instead of mackin'. Doing something positive with our paper stacking instead of acting like we packing. We glorify bullsh!t, and wonder why we still lacking...This is Cocktails coming from my cubicle All-Star venue. We are expecting large numbers for next week, so be safe and productive.

Identity Crisis

What you look like is not who you really are. I was in the nightclub sitting at the bar when I wrote this. Because it was hard for me to focus on you, but your clothes made me take notice. Men were swarming around you like locusts. Your shirt was low cut, and so were your jeans exposing the crack of your butt. I see you crack a smile as the next butt hole tries his Mack role, but truth be told. He's not buying you a drink; he's buying it for your clothes. It's the middle of the winter why are you exposed. But you get mad at me when I say it's some hoes…in this house. Hell, look at your blouse. I can see your nipple. Is it waiting for a mouth to latch on to it like a pacifier? Would that pacify her to know that people admire her look similar to a bachelor party flyer? What were you thinking when you chose that attire. That I would come up to you and ask if you were in the church choir. If you're clothes are a lie then don't be mad when you attract liars. What you look like is not who you really are. Why do you want to be a wannabee star? Everybody wants to be a Jaguar Wright, Alicia Keys, and Mary J. Blige. Would it oblige you if I complimented your fake hair and fake eyes? While inside your soul cries because you rely on your made up façade. When did you give up on God and start worshipping the man's rod as your staff. While you give people fake laughs and when I ask your story you only say half. Your self-esteem needs a bubble bath; think of all the different men in your life. Do the math, I'm sure that you will look back and be caught up in the Aftermath. Who sold you on this media witchcraft? When did you deviate to this strayed path? You look like the devil's depraved wrath of lust, he has murdered your trust, and you must not know that you are beautiful just being you. Being just who you are. Too bad, what you look like is not who you really are. Identity Crisis…This is Cocktails coming from my home cubicle self esteem seminar (classes are filling up).

Problem Solving

People are always too quick to identify a problem. However, it's a long painstaking process to solve them. And the stress activated your stomach acid to create a solvent. Plop, plop, fizz, fizz over the counter pills in alcohol trying to dissolve them. You want to scream for help, but don't want to inconvenience people or involve them. Your children are acting like chimpanzees, and you want to evolve them. You see your baby daddies' face in all them. And pray that their recklessness and carelessness isn't in all them. But if they knew of your indiscretions and secrets it would appall them. That you got these 'baby boys' by Sean Pauling. Shaking that ass for cash like it was your calling. And the fathers didn't know your name like Alicia Keys and now you're Falling. Twice you were raped because they thought that you were stalling. And they treated you like their rented Escalade for fake balling. Your sign read, "I Rent Escapades" but you called it modeling. And eventually you couldn't tell the difference between groping and mauling. You couldn't distinguish between an angel and a goblin. So you hit your knees for both, praying and gobbling. In the club, acting stuck up and hob knobbing, instead of at home parenting and cradle rocking. Weed and alcohol graduated to freebasing and rocking. The problem escalated to stealing and robbing. In the 'Hood' still looking for your 'Robin'. But constant dodging from problem solving turned your eye from the Sparrow, because you only learned how to Swallow. And constant abortions and hard living burned your womb hollow. What an example for your young boys to follow. Their idea of a mother, wife, and queen came from videos and Showtime at the Apollo. Their street 'Creed' taught them to fight like Apollo. Pow, straight to the moon, without using the Apollo. The moon wasn't the pie face that they know. They know hoes, blow, bootleg clothes, back roads, and values that are shallow. The product of being raised in shadows. This chapter is far from closed. What are the solutions now that the problems are exposed?...This is Cocktails coming from my home cubicle of ghetto fairytales. We still aren't out of the woods.

Pardon My Arrogance

Pardon my arrogance, but I'm looking for someone that I can put my heir against..put my hair against your breast. No offense, but I'm looking for someone with whom I can share my inheritance. Actually, I just want you to give me a chance. Maybe there is something in your life that I can enhance. I know that I might not be much at first glance, but look again. I have the characteristics to be your best friend, your next in-law kin, someone on who you can depend, someone with who you don't have to pretend. This initial conversation is where our relationship begins so...can we talk? Why are relationships going to hell with gasoline draws and propane panties? Why can't the good men and good women convene in an intimate spot without the facades and alter egos? Women, why are you settling? Men why are we acting up? No, switch that. Women, why are you building walls up, forcing the brothers that mean well to give up. These are the views of Cocktails, and not necessarily those of the Live Poets Society. Let it go. Be who you are and make that person accept you for who you are instead of who you want them to be. If you kick it and find out that you don't match, move on. Don't waste the other person's time trying to light wet wood with two sticks (old country saying). Maybe the divorce rate wouldn't be so high if we were honest with ourselves and our significant other from the beginning.(whoooaa, Cocktails don't hurt 'em). It's me again broadcasting from my cubicle dating game (the black Chuck Woolery, please believe it).

Never Settle

With spring love is in the air. Too bad that nobody cares. I see too many women wallowing in despair instead of trying to repair what we hold dear. Dear to whom it may concern. I'm concerned because I see the number of times that you've been burned. And what I've learned is that instead of feeling spurned, take those lessons as earned, and stop thinking that life is like "As the World Turns". Now you look at men like germs, but the ones that are pimping you don't have gold teeth and perms. You stay in dirt like worms, and then wonder why your daughter is off the hook. All she had to do was look and see what you presented, and those lessons she took. Put down the Iyanla and Oprah book, and learn how to cook. Stop worrying how men look and see how he treats you. If he beats you then it would beseech you to not open the door when he comes to greet you. Get out of the pressure cooker, because he probably can't stand the heat too. Love does not mean that he has to defeat you. You are more than a conqueror and your femininity has a farther reach too. God always has something to teach you. I know that you think that the world is out to eat you. But trust me, there are still some good brothers out there, and we can't wait to meet you…This is Cocktails coming from my dating game home cubicle. Respect starts with self.

Clarity

Ladies what's the disparity. I'm trying to get some clarity. Find-
ing healthy African American relationships is a rarity, and I'm love
sick trying to find someone to marry me. You said that you would
carry me until they bury me. Now I'm sitting here living through
old love movies vicariously. If communication is key, then I can't
find the lock. Because you have a brick wall up and a mental
block. While your biological clock warrants that you have flocks.
Your psychological lock box has warrants on almost every block.
Wanted: Will the real you please stand up. Because I would hate
to think that when you pee you stand up. You have more ice in your
veins than the Stanley Cup. And I Marvel like Stan Lee, so put
your superhero up. You're a black widow spider man, wrapping
super gyros up. Sucking men dry like super slurpee cups. Call me
Gerber baby, eat me and burp me up. Or Lever 2000, work me
and lather me up. You're not a slut, just misguided with men.
Because a grown man would want to have what is within. But
within this modern society, it taught you what it takes to win. That
Baby Phat isn't for the fat, but for the thin. You should wear a lot of
makeup because you should hate your skin. Be a baby momma
because you shouldn't know your kin. If you can't find a man at
church, at least you know your sin. But you'll find a man in the
club, because he bought your Hen. And you brought your friend
along, looking for the same thing. She's married too, but took off
her wedding ring. Because her husband has a mistress and spent
the offering. This is a black cancer in black relationships and it's
often seen. Recycled from your parents as a rotten gene. Often
airing your dirty laundry trying to keep your cotton clean. I mean.
Ladies what's the disparity I'm trying to get some clarity. Finding
healthy African American relationships is a rarity, and I'm love sick
trying to find someone to marry me. You said that you would carry
me until they bury me. Now I'm sitting here living through old love
movies vicariously. To Be Continued...This is Cocktails coming
from my Turner South home cubicle. Don't fall into the norm.

Have We Let You Down?

Lord, have we let you down since the civil rights fight? Something just ain't right. There are supposed to be major improvements in our plight. It used to be illegal for us to read and write. Now our youth frown on being able to read and write. And the cops are still waiting on us to mess up, so they can read us our rights. I hope people read what I write. Lord, lead our light. I watch footage of us protesting with all our might, because we knew that we were created equal in your sight. Now we think we're doing alright because the Klan doesn't visit our homes at night. They dangle a little bit of success at us, because they know we'll bite. And what's deep is I'm not talking about white. I'm talking about mentality. We forgot when we used our resources and bartering to compensate for a salary. Naturally thick sistas are counting calories. Us having to remember history by visiting an art gallery. We have no central theme in which we can rally. Sure we have some success stories, but still a majority are doing badly. Sadly, no one will agree. Because a lot of these "uppity people" have gotten degrees. And forgotten about slavery decrees. I've been in conversations that you wouldn't believe. Because they are standing on our ancestors back and they can't breathe. We walk around and talk as if they didn't bleed. Like it was easy for them to be freed. Like if it was us then we would have taken the lead. Please. All I see is greed. Our people taking what we want, instead of instilling what we need. So it is with this I plead. Black History didn't start in February, what are you doing for your people in the future to read?...This is Cocktails coming from my home cubicle of book reports. If they wrote a book on your life, what would it say?

It's About That Time

It's about that time. The reason that we stood in those long lines.
The reason that our people spent tireless hours holding picket
signs. The reason that they don't respect our minds. The reason
that they want to keep us deaf, dumb, and blind. The reason that
they want to keep our sight hind. The reason that our polling places
are hard to find. The reason that we stay on our grind. It's about
that time. Forty Years ago they didn't want to cater to our kind.
Forty years later we are still trying to break the ties that bind. They
still think our strength lies in fried chicken and watermelon rinds.
Cracked out hoods and weed vines. Rap music and so called
video dimes. Low income and violent crimes. It's about that time.
Let your freedom ring and chime. It's time to clean out the sleaze
and slime. Your voice can't be silent like a mime. These are the
same people that had your families swinging from pines. And their
outrageous ego still has them habitually crossing the line. That's
why they try to disenfranchise us and give us federal fines. They
don't think that we are a factor and will stay behind. How could
you possibly allow Bush to sit in the oval office four more years and
recline, line his pockets at the expense of America's decline and be
fine? It's about that time...

State of Mind

Our psychological state is poverty stricken. Our spirit is like a post
war Iraq that has been obviously stricken. We wonder why our
plights are disease stricken. Forgive us God for our awkward
living. Gay Marriages has the church and state splitting. Queer Eye
for the Straight Guy has men acting soft like kittens. Am I metro
sexual if I wear shirts that are form fitting and cross my legs during
conversations while I'm sitting? What if I eat overgrown chicken
that has our kids overgrown, but it's finger licking. Now our
teachers see kids as finger licking and touch them with their mittens.
Then tell them it's in the name of You, and to tell anyone else is
forbidden. Our everyday seems like an "Underworld", and I weave
through Vampires and Werewolves trying not to be bitten. I'm
trying to throw up the peace sign, but my middle finger keeps
sticking. Way before Nas was spitting, "It Was Written", we
listened. Way before our crosses glistened, you were risen. Now
we scroll our records by prison. We glorify gluttonous living on
records and keep it real by going to prison. It doesn't matter as
long as we are certified platinum by a prism. These strange seasons
are starting to symbolize a cataclysm. Time seems like it's speeding
up like a time bomb ticking. Our ideologies are sick and morals
suck like a prostitute tricking. I can't hide from the problems, but
sometimes I want to get while it's good for the getting. Is this "As
Good As it Gets"? I'm not Jack Nicholson, so I can't deal with
these Jokers when I'm placing my bets. That's why I stay in Your
House, because the house wins every time. There are many
mansions, and I'm waiting for mine. But the devil keeps baiting me
with quick dimes. Thank you for helping me to discern between
quick lines and friends for lifetime. I thought that I couldn't be a
spiritual millionaire, but you gave me two more lifelines. Now I
honor You by giving my congregation life rhymes. Thank you for
blessing me with words to allow my light to shine.

Looking Back

Looking through my old things and photos feeling like Frodo waiting for the Lord to Ring. Ever since the Two Towers left the scene, I've felt like Return of the King. Fighting between good and evil like Gollum and Smeagle, back when my people used to keep their goods in the Regal. Until the law's snoopy beagle did a search and seizure illegal. Now he's grounded like an ill eagle with clipped wings and nursing sores. Won't let him soar over drug wars but we memorize movie clips of drug lords and recite it like scripture. We ball out of control like excited pitchers. Our kids are all out of control like raggedy ceiling fan fixtures. Going around in a circle but you can't feel the breeze. We go around in popular circles and contract the same disease. I know people with street sense and book sense and God considers it the same degrees. He gives us a choice of our retirement, because the environment won't have the same degrees. We blame decree for our unequal entities. We half step and ask for sympathy, but to a homeless man we have no empathy. This is a homeless land, and we are increasing in enemies. We caught Saddam and want to give him the death penalty. What will God give you when you stand before His Jury?

We Sick

We Sick. Sick as a people, sick as a race. Sick as a country, sick
as a world. Sick in the body, sick in the face. Sick as a boy, sick
as a girl. Sick as a church, sick in education. Sick as a family, sick
as friends. Sick in teachings, sick around the nation. Sick with
ourselves, too sick to make amends. Sick with our values, sick
with our morals. Sick with our actions, sick with our thoughts.
Sick with our loyalty, sick with our laurels. Sick with society, sick
and distraught. Sick and tired of being sick and tired. Sick of the
situation, sick of the job. Sick of pity, sick of wallowing in mire.
Sick of bullsh!t, sick of people trying to rob. Sick in the mental,
sick in the soul. Sick in our wants, sick in our needs. Sick in
speech, sick in goals. Sick in messages, too sick to take heed.
Sick in pornography, sick in destruction. Sick in the struggle, sick in
the game. Sick in dependencies, sick in our functions. Sick in our
means, sick in our aims. We nauseating, ill, putrid, despicable. Not
caring, stony, empty, cold. The acts of evil are becoming critical.
Life span dropping, no one left to be old. I'm sick of saying we
sick but, We Sick. No for real...something is wrong with humanity.
My man stacked up over 100 bodies in his crematory because he
said his machine was broken?!!!! Man, use an old fashioned gas
can and a match, do something, anything, don't just leave them
there! The woman is on trial this week for drowning her five
children. The state wants the death penalty. Her defense says she
is insane. Hmmm, let me see...she drowned all five children me-
thodically, then called 911 to come get them. You make the call.
This is Cocktails broadcasting live from my cubical psychiatric ward
(it's hard to type in this straight jacket).

Chapter 5
Drink 5

Cubicle Confessions

(Compilation of Writings in Corporate America)

Working Man's Zinfandel

Ingredients

1 shot Tequilla, 1 shot Scotch, 1/2 shot cinnamon schnapps, 1/2 shot peach schnapps, 1 can Sprite

Mixing Instructions

Add shots of liquor to the glass. Fill with Sprite.

The Good Die Young

The Good Die Young...No one realizes how profound most cliché's are. As most of you know, the singer/actress/entertainer Aaliyah passed on Saturday night. Our prayers go out to her close friends and family. It really was kind of crazy, because I woke up on Sunday morning with a renewed heart. I celebrated my birthday on yesterday. While I was thanking the creator for another year with my health and mental awareness, he took another one of his children home. It brings reality crashing into your face with all of its ugliness and horror coupled with beauty and grace. I went to church with my mother, looking at her vibrant and full of life at a late age, then took notice of the newborns and children running around Sunday school. Tomorrow is promised to no one. As soon as you're born, you take a number to die, from SIDS to old age. When God calls your number, what legacy will you have left with your time? I'm not even questioning anyone's spirituality, or relationship with whomever you chose to worship. I'm speaking of the borrowed time that you have on this earth. Maximize your life to the fullest. Time is something that you will never be able to get back. This is Cocktails mixing those lifeline elements on your Monday.

Bamboozled

I finally saw "Bamboozled" yesterday. I know that I am kind of late, but the commentary never is. Being an "entertainer", or even trying to break into the industry comes with its "rights of passage". I have always loved being on stage, but what do people see when I am up there? What thoughts are going through their heads? My fraternity brothers (A PHI till I die) and I used to joke about how we would "coon" for the audience when we were stepping...but we never lost a show...coincidence? What drives you when you are watching our people on stage? Are they cooning or performing? Is there a fine line? It's not limited to just the stage, because life is a stage, and we are merely the players. Black or white, are you "shuffling" for society? SUV's, houses, cars, economic status, how did you achieve it? Today I am challenging everyone to take an honest inventory within, and for every virtue you find missing try and weave it in. No man or woman is greater than the next one. Most of us are a paycheck away from being that homeless person on the street. Humble yourself, and thank God for your blessings. This is Cocktails broadcasting from my cubicle minstrel show.

War

War, huh, good God y'all. What is it good for? Absolutely
nothing...On the tailwind of destruction and mayhem, America is
calling and rallying for support from a demoralized nation. We are
fighting an enemy with no face. Our attitude is to retaliate on
everyone that we THINK might have done the unthinkable to our
native soil. Gut check. Wake up call. Lightbulb! God is trying to
tell us something. We have heard all of the Revelations,
Nostradamus, and Conspiracy Theories known to man. However,
the fact remains that thousands of people have perished senselessly,
and the world remains spinning on it's axis. We have witnessed a
part of history. This is our Pearl Harbor. Is the solution to take out
their country? We know that our president has an itchy trigger
finger. No, undeniably America has bigger guns and funds for war,
hell, we gave them over half of what they posses. We trained them
on how to assassinate us. We created our own Frankenstein, and it
has turned on the Mad Scientist. Agape Love is essential at this
juncture of our own self meditation. Through death we see life. If
you have beef with someone, squash it. If someone is harassing
you, pray for them. Tuesday really revealed the pettiness that
dwells within us on a daily basis. I'm not going to patronize the
situation any further than it has been in the media. My final com-
ment on the situation is GET RIGHT. With that being said, Live
Poets is moving forward. God willing we are still standing, as
well as you should.

Back to Life

Back to Life, Back to Reality...Have we ever left? Will we ever wake up from this dream, or have we been living in our own nightmare that dreaming can not take away? Bush is telling America to go back to their normal lives on today, but never again will our lives be the same. We have lost friends, associates, comrades, relatives, and the body count is building on a daily basis. I'll tell you what a normal life is...God, Family, Friends (Fraternity or Sorority too, if you are a member), in that order. Add a healthy dose of goodwill towards mankind, and you have a pretty good "Recipe of Existence" brewing. We have gotten too complex in our lifestyles. The stock market is faltering, chemical warfare, disease, broken families, insolent children, economically driven churches, bullsh!t media tactics, Madam Cleo, privacy invasion, racial profiling, the list goes on, and on, and...what are we to do? Remember when your word was your bond, bartering was a form of currency, villages raised children, children were respectful to elders, doing the right thing was cool, we actually gave a damn about each other. Does it take a national emergency to regain God, Patriotism, Compassion, Intellect, Humility, and most of all R-E-S-P-E-C-T for one another? Today go back to your life, the way it was supposed to be. This is Cocktails marching into your emails from my cubicle military base.

Now I Lay me Down to Sleep

Now I lay me down to sleep. I pray the Lord my soul to keep. If I should die before I wake...I probably licked an anthrax envelope trying to pay my bills! I am never paying another bill again, and if the collection agency calls, I'll tell him I'm scared to open my mail. Come on people, who is the sick, sadistic creep (for lack of a better word) adding to America's misery and strife for no apparent reason. I was frying chicken last night, and accidentally mailed something with some flour residue. The next thing I know, FBI was busting down my door, evacuating my subdivision! No but seriously, chemical warfare or chemical warscare? We are basically swinging like a girl with our eyes closed at the enemy. Are we still fighting them? Then again, who's them? You know who they are...they are THEY. Which is basically nobody. My Wag the Dog theory this week is Bush is diverting attention from the real problem (of course he did a good job, because I forgot what the real problem was). This is Cocktails broadcasting from my CDC certified cubicle. Keep loving, eventually it will overpower the hate.

Who We Be

They don't know. WHO WE BEEEEE!!! We be the underground sound moving the concrete under your feet with our soulful beats. We be keeping our lives together, gritting our teeth, because we are tough as leather. We be braving the cold weather, while our boss is misbehaving, dodging corporate bullets, email soul saving. We be praying, while our people are still under the rubble, watching money being given to the ones with benefits, while the underprivileged are still in trouble. We be balancing our financial bubble, hoping it doesn't pop, watching our stock, saying please stop the drop. We be inching through road blocks, racial profiling from cops has us thrown in jail for detox from .086, defrocked, but still not shocked. We be learning from Biggie and Tupac, but still cry out thug, three strikes from drugs, cold compassion has us longing to be hugged. Do you see who we be? They don't know, or can't see, that we be COMMUNITY. And I be Cocktails, mixing those email scribes for your Thursday Vibes.

You Can't See Me

Wooooooo(my scary voice) BOO! I'm a ghost...no, I'm a black man in America. You can't see me!! I lurk in the dark alleys of the hood, waiting to jump out, just like the white sheets jumped out on me to take my soul. My silhouette is permanently stained on the jail cell wall, spirit broken like the stained glass in the cathedral church...and they are still haunting me. You can't see me, I walk by you everyday, searching for vindication, because they told me that I am of this earth, but not for this earth. BOO!! I'm in the executive board room, floating aimlessly away, because I am a token of the ghastly things that are unspoken. I have the sixth sense (third eye), because I see dead people everyday, soul clapping in the club, with no soul. When the music dies, so do I, because I spent my child support on this female I was trying to holla at. I'm harder to find than Waldo, because I don't mentor, parent, obligate, reciprocate, lead, and accept my God given talents and responsibilities. You can't see me, I'm transparent. I am seen but not heard. What makes you (your spirit), whole? This is Cocktails haunting your emails for the Halloween week.

I Have A Dream

A Dream Deferred...I Have a Dream...no for real, I really had a
dream waiting for my car to be fixed this morning. (why is the labor
always more than the part?) As I drifted in and out of conscious-
ness, listening to a well put together Memorial Service for Dr. King,
thoughts wafted through my brain. Politically, spiritually, racially,
and otherwise it was a great unification rally. However, me always
being the devil's advocate, I wondered what would tomorrow's
sunrise bring? These speakers (same speech different delivery)
spoke passionately of Dr. King's vision and what he stood for.
Tomorrow, will their actions match their words? I equivocate this
modern day dream to my student loans (metaphorically of
course). We have built up this big debt to society, and to the
community by taking out this loan on humanity (Dr. King's vision).
But when it is time to pay it back, we defer our payments, accruing
this large amount of interest (mentoring, community service). We
plan, or intend to start paying it back, but keep deferring our
payment to society and family because of various trivial reasons.
One day we look up, and the vision is lost because there is so
much interest that has buried the original loan. When are you going
to start making payments? This is Cocktails broadcasting from my
million cubicle march. (Everybody walk out...just kidding)

Training Day

As I sit wasting away in training, I started to analyze this training concept. Reason being, I am being retrained on something that I train other people for. First of all, the first wave of training is for management. This is to teach them what they already should have known at the time of hiring. Then, the management in turn is unleashed on the floor to exert their new expertise on the associates. The associates, trusting that the manager knows best, feels inferior because they are obviously "ignorant" to the manager's knowledge (which is minimal). Then the associate goes to the same training that the management received. The associate then finds out that the manager knows just as much as them, if not less. Disgruntled disrespect then sets in at your oppressor, making you the aggressor. Switch that to real life. You let someone dictate to you what their opinion of your life should be, based on what someone else told them. Seek your own knowledge and truth. If you listen to another person's "professional" opinion, then you will always be living in their dominion. Break the shackles and breathe. This is Cocktails teaching from my EBT (Email Based Training) Cubicle.

March Madness

March Madness...Yes, Yes, N D FACE! (Coming to America, for the movie impaired). March Madness has begun and the leading basketball teams from their perspective conferences will embark upon their NCAA Tournament Journey. The winner is to receive the coveted NCAA Championship for the year. Me being a metaphorical man (is that a word?), I have always translated athletic competition into real life prose. We are all placed in brackets in society. The lowest seed (poor, underprivileged) always has to play the highest seed (rich, political) and win to gain advancement towards the next round. Of course, the highest seed is favored to win, because it is clearly the better team on paper (socially, economically, etc). However, in every tournament, a lower seed, always upsets the chosen and highly favored champion. Why? Because of heart, and being the underestimated underdog, the lower seed prevails. Sometimes it isn't always good to be the top seed, because someone will always be gunning for you. Where are you seeded in your life? Do you practice every day to improve yourself, and not to be beaten? Win or go home. Some never make it to the big dance. Take everyday like a day in the tournament. If you are not at your best, you could be beaten. This is Cocktails reporting from my cubicle press box (he shoots, he scores).

Artificial Intelligence

Artificial Intelligence...I think therefore I am. They think therefore they are. If they think that I am and I think they are, which they really are, are not, are we really we...I think (I've gone cross-eyed). Who thinks for you? Is it you? Or a derivative of you placed in artificial intelligence? Maybe we are artificial intelligence, because we are constructed of neurons, nerves, and energy, much like a computer. Has the human become so stupid, as to where the computer has actually outsmarted us? (The student has become the teacher) When was the last time you made a decision without the use of a palm pilot, email, organizer, software program, etc. Our brains are atrophying and we don't even realize it, because we think that computers are making us smarter, because we taught them to be more efficient in our lives. The more we tell them, the dumber we get. Quick, add 217+345 (put that calculator down). Don't forget to exercise your brain every now and then. Dependency on machines coupled with a consistent regiment of drugs and alcohol, are making us prime candidates for...artificial intelligence (Hello Hal, for my 2001 folk). This is Cocktails hooked up to my virtual email cubicle program. (I'm really not here)

Pledging Allegiance

(Everyone please stand for the Pledge of Allegiance) I pledged
allegiance. We've been had, by the divided states of embarrass-
ment. And to the Republic, which we can't stand. A divided
nation, help us God, to be better individuals. This Liberty disgusts
us all. (Where are the Democrats when you need them?) Y'all
gon' make me lose my mind up in here, up in here. The church and
state are supposed to be separate. The nation is supposed to be
under God. Well if the states are under the nation, which is under
God, but the state is not under God then the nation should not be
under God...right? Well that means, that the currency that we use is
null and void, because the currency is In God We Trust, which we
really don't trust because that would be a conflict of interest with
the individuals that would be Under God, that do not want to be
under God. (I've gone cross-eyed again). F the Pledge. It's bigger
than that. Think, schools removed God, state has removed God,
now the nation has removed God. And we are still asking God to
help and save us?!! Get right, God is trying to tell us something.
This is Cocktails pledging my email allegiance to Live Poets (Our
stock is worth more than Worldcom!)

Fired

THE DAY I WAS FIRED.
Guess who's back. Did you miss me? Running along the beach
throwing a Frisbee. How serene could this be? Having Brazilian
women kiss me on…the cheek. Por Quito Portuguese, how do I
speak? However the situation is far from bleak. To think this
Southside Houston native from Mo City, off of Ridgecreek, would
end up in another country lying on the beach. With spoken words I
preach, we all have goals to reach. Stop being picked off by
obstacle snipers and each one teach. Build strong relationships like
Preach and Cochise. War is global, but in your mind have peace.
And patriotism is noble, but what is loyalty without the belief. If
your desire is dormant, go ahead and order your wreath. Because
your subconscious is dead, and even your conscious is six feet
deep. I hustle and struggle so hard that sometimes I want to weep.
But hope floats, and blessings come in heaps. And a man sows
what he reaps, and it's not what you cop, but what you can keep.
Guess who took that leap…This is Cocktails coming from my home
base office. Incoming newsflash! I WILL NO LONGER BE
BROADCASTING FROM THE CUBICLE. (The sun baked my
brain, and I couldn't find my office :-) Pray for me, as I have
stepped out on faith (actually nudged).

Afterword

So there you have it. One down, infinity to go. To those that read this cover to cover, thank you. To those that skimmed this, and now it's collecting dust in your bookcase, thank you. The beautiful thing of stepping outside of your comfort zone, is once you do it, you're like, "Hey, this wasn't bad. I could have done it sooner." So now that we've broken the seal on the Cocktails Commentaries' series, expect more from your boy. Hopefully you see my growth and maturity through my writing in the early stages of my career. The heart never runs out of ink, so as long as God allows me, I will continue to expose my soul on paper. Who knows. Hopefully one day, I'll have marriage, kids, maybe even grandkids commentaries to add to the repertoire! Only time will reveal. Until then, have a drink on me. Mentally, Spiritually, and Physically. Holla at ya boy!

Afterglow

Ingredients

1 part Grenadine, 4 parts Orange Juice, 4 Parts Pineapple Juice

Mixing Instructions

Mix. Serve over ice.

Printed in the United States
50049LVS00006B/301-402